MARKETING

The Beginners Guide to Making Money Online with Social Media for Small Businesses

ALEX NKENCHOR UWAJEH

Legal Disclaimers

CONTENTS

INTRODUCTION

Social media sites offer a massive range of benefits for small businesses. Not only are they a low-cost way to build brand awareness about your business and your products, but they're also an excellent way to attract new customers.

If you get your marketing strategy right, social media platforms can give you direct access to your current customers. They also give you a way to reach out and connect with prospective customers.

There is also the advantage of being able to monetize your social media marketing efforts. Not only are you able to promote your existing products, but there are some ways you can generate additional revenue from your online marketing efforts.

The result of earning extra income from your social media marketing on top of generating more sales is more profits for your business overall.

Of course, the key to success with social media marketing is to understand the right ways to leverage each social media platform to your advantage.

Are you ready to get started? Let's get into it...

MARKETING FOR SMALL BUSINESSES

Before you dive into the deep end and start posting your marketing messages all over your social media sites, it's important to take a bit of time to create a solid strategy.

Your objective is to attract traffic to your website or

landing page and then convert that traffic into new leads or increased sales. After all, there's no point generating loads of traffic if those visitors aren't converting into sales or leads.

In order to really build a strong marketing strategy, you first need to know a bit about the people who are likely to become your customers.

Behind every successful social media campaign is a clearly-thought-out strategy designed to help you connect with the right people who fit within your target audience. In order to build your strategy the right way, you first need to define your audience.

Define Your Target Audience

In order to create marketing messages that engage your customers and entice them to buy from you, it's important to understand the types of people within your target audience.

Create a character profile of your ideal customer. Try to determine the age bracket, gender, profession, location, and interests of the people in your target audience.

In some cases, you might find that your audience's characteristics might overlap in some areas. You might also find that some of your audience might require a different marketing angle than others.

For example, your target market might be made up of a majority of females aged between 34 and 44. However, you may still have a large cross-section of customers who are male and aged between 28 and 34.

If your initial research shows you a variance in the type of people within your target audience, you have the opportunity to slant your marketing to appeal directly to those different characteristics.

When you have defined the people you believe fall into your target audience, you're in a stronger position to start working on the right marketing message to reach them effectively.

Define Pain Points

Based on the characteristics you worked out when you were defining your audience, think about what key problems or issues those people face. In marketing terms, this is known as defining 'pain points'.

For example, let's assume you're selling dog training products. You might identify your customer's pain point as being unable to train their dog properly. Your solution might be to offer them your unique training product.

Sounds easy, right?

Not quite. You see, your dog training product may not be the exact solution your customer is searching for. Behind every customer's surface pain point is usually a deeper pain point that needs to be explored in more detail. You need to dig a bit deeper to be sure your product is the right solution for your customer's issue.

After all, if your dog training product is focused on helping the owner teach a dog to walk nicely on a leash and your customer simply wants some help with basic obedience in the home, your product no longer solves that customer's issue.

Here's an imaginary conversation between you and a customer about digging deeper to find the true pain point you want to uncover:

> **You**: Why do you want dog training products?
>
> **Customer**: To get my dog to behave better.
>
> **You**: Why do you want your dog to behave better?
>
> **Customer**: So I can have people over without him jumping all over them.
>
> **You**: Why do want to keep the dog inside when you have people over?
>
> **Customer**: Because I want my new girlfriend to like my dog.
>
> **You**: Why do you want your girlfriend to like your dog?

Customer: Because if she's going to hang around in future, I need her and the dog to get along.

Okay, it's a bit over-simplified, but in this example you've actually uncovered four different pain points.

1. The main issue is getting the dog to behave better
2. The main need is allowing the dog to remain inside when guests come over
3. The desired outcome is getting the dog and the girlfriend to get along nicely
4. The true pain point is, worrying that his badly-behaved dog might drive guests away.

Ideally, you should try to work out at least three pain points for each character type in your target audience profiles.

Hold imaginary conversations with your customers to find how your products can help them find solutions to their pain points. Head over to your favorite search engine and look for frequently asked questions related to similar products within your industry.

Look for what issues or concerns your customers are talking about on social media platforms or in community groups or forums. Really focus hard on defining those pain points, because solving those problems for your customers is the key to your success.

When you center your marketing strategy on your customer's pain points, your conversion rate will increase dramatically.

Create Your Marketing Messages

Once you've determined your pain

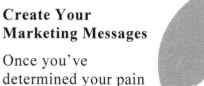

points, you're in a great position to work out how your business and your products can help customers solve or overcome them.

After all, research shows that people are often more motivated by fear of loss than hope of gain. People are hard-wired to avoid pain, so successful marketers know they need to offer solutions to people's pain points.

Your marketing messages need to reinforce in your customer's minds that you understand what they need. You need to illustrate their pain point and then demonstrate how your product solves that issue.

When you've worked through your marketing messages, it's time to put them to good use.

DOMINATE SOCIAL MEDIA PLATFORMS

It's common for many small business owners to choose one or two primary social media platforms and try to focus their marketing efforts on those.

However, almost every social media site serves a different purpose within your marketing strategy. Each social media platform has a different primary audience. They have different methods of imparting information, differing focuses, and use varying forms of media to get your message across.

For example, YouTube is solely focused on video sharing, while Pinterest is focused more on visual imagery. Twitter limits you to a maximum of 140 characters, while LinkedIn allows you to post entire blog posts or articles.

Then there are audience differences to consider. For example, the largest age demographic of YouTube users is aged between 24 and 34. By comparison, a massive 53% of users on Instagram are aged 18 to 29, while the largest age demographic of users on LinkedIn is aged 30 to 49.

Of course, there are also gender differences to take into account as well. 56% of users on LinkedIn are male, while Pinterest's primary audience is female.

Then there are sites that appeal more strongly to the rapidly expanding millennial audience. A whopping 45% of SnapChat users are aged between 13 and 24.

It's important to take the time to learn and understand the differences between various platforms. You're in a stronger position to direct your efforts on the right channels that way.

Besides, if you don't understand the differences between each platform, how will you know which ones are best suited to add into your marketing strategy?

It's not necessary for you to create business profiles or pages on every social media platform out there. But it is important to choose the right ones to reach your target audience effectively.

Getting People to Follow You on Social Media

In order to get your website visitors to follow you on your chosen social media accounts, it's important you display the social icons you use for your business on all your pages and posts.

Include a call to action on the bottom of each blog post and ask readers to actively follow you on their preferred social media platform. This gives your visitors the option to choose which platform they want to use if they want to see more updates from you.

For example, if you use Facebook, Pinterest, and Google Plus, ask people to follow you on those platforms.

It's a good idea to include sharing buttons on all your website posts. People like to share interesting content on their own social profiles, so make it easy for them.

Coordinating Your Social Channels

Treating each different social media platform as a stand-alone effort could potentially limit your marketing campaign's success. Ideally, your strategy should be to work your social networks together so they all contribute to helping you achieve your goals.

Of course, if you're like most small business owners, you simply don't have the time to log into multiple social networks to post updates.

You do have the option of simply clicking your own share buttons at the end of each post to send them to each of your social media sites. Your social platforms are instantly

MARKETING

I

**The Beginners Guide to Making Money Online
with Social Media for Small Businesses**

However, there's a lot more involved in a successful social media marketing campaign than just keeping your social platforms updated.

You also need an effective way to manage and track analytics for each of your social media profiles as well.

That's where the right social media management tools can be invaluable for every small business owner.

Services like Hootsuite (www.hootsuite.com) give you access to a full suite of tools designed to enhance audience engagement. The service is free for up to three social media platforms, but a monthly fee applies if you want to integrate more than three.

You can use the service to streamline your social marketing campaigns and increase your visibility across a broad range of social channels easily, including Facebook, Twitter,

LinkedIn, Google Plus, Instagram, SnapChat, YouTube, and many others.

As you can manage many social profiles on the same dashboard, you can respond to messages or replies to your posts right there in the same place, without having to log into separate profiles to see who's contacted you. HootSuite also lets you schedule content so that it is automatically posted at pre-determined times to ensure your social profiles are kept active.

The objective of your social media platforms is to drive people to your website so they can buy your product. Once they arrive on your website, it's your job to lead them through your sales funnel until they buy something from you and become paying customers.

Your job is to determine which social media networks and platforms are best suited to reaching the people in your target audience.

QUALITY CONTENT IS KING!

No matter how awesome your ability to update your social media profiles regularly might be, without quality content your efforts will be largely ignored.

People are still drawn to engaging content that is relevant to them. If your social media updates are all self-promotional, your followers will soon start thinking of them as not being useful to them.

Think about this: if your followers don't find your content interesting, why would they share it with others?

The simple answer is: they won't.

The key to success with social media marketing is providing great content that your followers find useful in some way.

It doesn't matter whether your target audience's version of 'useful' means educational, informative, entertaining, or enlightening. Your job is to find and deliver great content that keeps your audience engaged.

Remember, people would much rather share interesting, useful, or entertaining content than sales-type promotional updates about your products or services.

Finding Your Content

Content is the basis of all social marketing. Unfortunately, if you're like most other small business owners, you simply won't have the time to trawl through the Internet searching for good content to share.

You also probably won't have the time to sit down and write your own awesome content or produce compelling video presentations every day either.

You do have options available to help lighten the work load.

Head over to the social media profiles of other businesses in your niche. Take note of the questions people ask or any concerns they have in the comments they leave on posts. Then use those questions or concerns to form helpful content you can post on your own site.

Sites like Feedly (http://feedly.com/) aggregate content from various sources and organize it for you, which makes it much easier to find the types of content you want to add to your marketing strategy.

Feedly also allows you to integrate your account into other social tools, such as Sprout Social (http://sproutsocial.com/features/social-media-publishing), so you can easily share the articles you find.

Likewise, Canva (https://www.canva.com/) is a web-based design tool that lets you create images you can share across your social networks. The site features a whole section of social media templates that let you create posts that are already correctly sized to suit each different social media network you want to use.

You might also use Piktochart (http://piktochart.com/) to create your own infographics, especially if you want to deliver data-driven content out to your followers.

User Generated Content

It's possible that many small businesses can harness the power of social media to get their followers to generate plenty of content for them.

For example, a few years ago Starbucks asked their followers to draw on their Starbucks cups and submit the photos as entries. The prize was that the company would create a template for a new limited edition cup from the winning entry.

The contest saw almost 4,000 images submitted in the space of three weeks, which kept their social media pages busy, active, and populated with strong branding – all of which was generated by users.

Your followers will often be happy to provide content for you – as long as you tell them what you want. Just be sure you match your promotional theme to your audience.

Here are some quick ideas for encouraging user-generated content:

- Ask your followers to upload photos to your business profile page of themselves doing something pertinent to your chosen topic matter.

- Ask them to create a funny or cool saying or a slogan based on one of your own images and see how many interesting replies you get.

- Ask your followers to upload an image or graphic that features your logo or brand in some way.

Be creative with your requests – and you can be sure your followers will be equally as creative with the content they provide.

Of course, once they've generated lots of content, you have the opportunity to repurpose it to create even more content.

You can choose the top three or four entries submitted by followers and repost these as a separate piece of content highlighting the winning entries.

You could create a separate post asking your followers to vote on your favorite three or four submissions to narrow down the winning options even further.

One of the best things about asking followers to create ideas for you is that you have the opportunity to learn what they think of your business, your brand, and your products based on their responses.

More Than Words

It's common for many small business owners to automatically associate 'content' with long, wordy articles or blog posts filled with lots of keywords. However, social media has expanded the meaning of content to also include other forms of visual media too.

With that in mind, your content might include some interesting or useful articles related to your business's niche or products published on your website or blog. Rather than just put a big chunk of text on your web pages, think about ways to improve visual appeal too.

Add images or graphics that help to illustrate your topic. Break up your text blocks with other types of content.

You aren't limited to just using articles or blog posts to get your message across. You might also intersperse your marketing messages across various social media channels with pertinent or relevant images, photos, infographics, memes, and videos that encourage your audience to interact with what you've posted in some way.

Keep your content interesting and vary the type of content you provide. After a while, your own analytics will reveal what type of content is attracting the most attention.

You will also be able to track the types of content that encourage your audience to click through to your website or landing page, or those that end up buying something from you.

Use your analytics to keep track of where your paying customers are coming from. Learn which content encourages people to share it among their own circles.

Take notice of what types of content get people responding to your messages. Then note which content gets largely ignored, or gets very little attention.

The results you find should shape the direction of your future marketing efforts.

Optimizing Your Content

Always remember that you still need to optimize your content to suit each different social network you're including in your marketing strategy.

For example: if you're posting a new article or blog post on your website, you can easily post a link to your content on some social media sites without problem, such as Facebook or LinkedIn or Google Plus.

However, other social platforms may require visual prompts to engage your audience. Add some interesting and enticing images that relate to your subject matter into your blog post. Use a simple editing tool to add the title of your blog post onto the primary image and share it to Instagram, SnapChat, or Pinterest.

Always think about the best way to let your audience know what your message is about at a glance. You have a far greater chance of engaging them.

Encouraging Interaction

Creating your content is just the beginning of your social media marketing efforts. It's equally as important to ensure every piece of content you include in your marketing strategy features share buttons that are clearly visible.

If people like what you're posting, they're more likely to share it around their own circles of friends or followers if the share button is right there under their noses.

Whenever you publish a new post, make sure you share it on your own social media sites first. That gets the share numbers started and makes it obvious to people that others find it useful enough to share it. You also remove the stigma of being the first to share something.

You also want to make it easy for your website visitors to follow you on social media sites. Be sure your social network icons are clearly visible somewhere on every page of your site.

There are handy plug-ins available that display all your social media icons if you're using Wordpress. You can have your icons displayed permanently down the side of each page, or across the top, or even in the side bar if you want.

You might even include a simple line at the
bottom of each post reminding people to share
it, or asking them to leave a comment or
opinion.

SOCIAL NETWORKING

Social media marketing involves much more than simply being active on your social networks. There's no point being really active on your social networks if no one buys anything from you.

Of course, there's also no point blasting self-promotional posts all over your social media profiles in an effort to attract attention.

The key is to create strong networks of people who are keenly interested in what you have to offer.

By now, you should have share buttons at the bottom of every post on your website or blog. You should also have clearly visible social media icons on your website encouraging people to follow you.

Building Your Social Networks

If your networks still aren't growing as quickly as you like, find new ways to entice people to follow or like you.

For example, you might mention that only VIP members of your Facebook page or Google Plus page or Twitter feed will receive coupon codes from time to time. Everyone loves the idea of a bargain or a discount, so it's likely that some people will begin following you on your social media sites to wait for the next coupon or promotional code or discount offer you post.

Remember, while those people might initially click 'Like' or 'Follow' just to get a discount, they also want to know that it's worth their time to stay with you.

Don't just blast promotional codes on your social networks. Really encourage some

interaction with your followers. Ask their
opinions and encourage feedback.

Offer plenty of useful tips and helpful content
that is relevant to your specific niche.

Whenever anyone leaves a comment, question,
or any type of feedback, make certain you
respond. Even if it's just to say thank you, it's
important that people recognize that their
feedback has been acknowledged.

Above all, take the time to welcome all your
new followers. Thank them for sharing your
content. Show your appreciation for their
efforts.

Networking to Your Advantage

Set aside a bit of time each day to leave a
helpful comment on a couple of Facebook
pages within the same or similar niche to
yours. It gets your Facebook business profile
out there and seen by others who are following
the same niche.

MARKETING

**The Beginners Guide to Making Money Online
with Social Media for Small Businesses**

If you're on Twitter, re-tweet interesting tweets you find from others talking about similar topics to yours. With Pinterest, look for great images that match your audience's interests and re-pin some.

If you're on LinkedIn, share links to other people's posts that you think your audience might find interesting. Join LinkedIn groups and participate in conversations.

The key is to use networks to enhance your authority and increase awareness of you and your brand.

MAKING MONEY ONLINE WITH SOCIAL MEDIA

The vast majority of social media marketing strategies are focused solely on increasing brand awareness and building up the number of prospective customers within your target audience.

Everything you would have done up until now with your social media marketing strategy is designed to increase your follower numbers and attract attention to your business's products or services.

The end result of building up so much awareness of your business on social media is intended to get people to click through to your landing page or your website so they eventually become paying customers.

However, did you know it's also possible to make money with social media?

A good example of using social media to generate sales is Dell Computers. Dell has a dedicated Twitter feed (@DellOutlet) that offers exclusive discounts to its 1.6 million followers. From time to time, the company issues a special coupon code offering 15% or 20% discount off their products, which has helped to generate more than $2 million in additional sales from people on their list.

If you don't want to use discount coupons as part of your promotional strategy, you can still use social media to increase sales of your own products.

For example, Facebook and Instagram allow you to set up a store right there on their sites relatively easily with just a few clicks. You can link your Facebook store to Shopify, while Instagram allows you to connect to InSelly to accept payments.

There are also apps out there, such as Shopify that make it easy to create an online store that can be promoted widely across a range of social media networks. Shopify also allows you to integrate an Amazon Webstore, an eBay store, or even an Etsy store so you can connect any Amazon or eBay listings you have to your storefront and display them across your social media channels.

Facebook and Twitter are ideal platforms for creating dedicated business pages where you can display your products, while sites like Instagram and Pinterest are almost largely image-driven. If your products lend themselves to interesting images that engage your audience, you can draw plenty of attention to them.

However, if you don't have your own products you still have plenty of options for making money. Affiliate marketing gives you access to a massive range of products across almost any market you can think of. Your job is to promote affiliate products to your followers. When someone buys something from you, the merchant pays you an affiliate commission.

Keep in mind that many social media sites won't allow you to post direct affiliate links in your posts or status updates. Instead, it's a wiser idea to direct followers to your landing page and focus on driving sales from there.

You can also use social media to develop new product lines. Building up a relationship with a reliable drop shipping company gives you access to products you can promote easily on your social media storefront.

Monetizing Social Media

Aside from selling your existing products and services, some social media platforms give you the opportunity to monetize your marketing efforts.

YouTube is perhaps the best known social media platform for generating revenue. You'll need to join the YouTube Partner Program in order to monetize your videos.

When you become a YouTube Partner, you effectively split any revenue earned by the ads shown during and before your video.

As more people view your videos and subscribe to your YouTube channel, the potential for earning more revenue increases. The key to increasing your video views is to work on ways to encourage people to share them on various social media sites.

Paid Sponsorship

The rise in popularity of some social media sites has allowed some users to generate huge incomes from paid sponsorships.

For example, 24-year-old Jerome Jarre began building 6-second videos and blasting them out to his 6 million followers on Vine, the Twitter-owned social media platform. From there, he shifted over to SnapChat and built up a staggering 1.3 million followers in just a few weeks. He's turned his social media following into a $100,000 income.

According to a story published in Business Insider, 24-year-old Cody Johns earns his entire living on Vine. His efforts on the social media side paid off his college tuition.

If you've built up a strong following on one of
your social media networks, you could easily
monetize that popularity with sponsors or
advertisers.

Video Marketing Strategies

Let's face it: videos are fun to watch and easy to digest. People who are short on time don't always want to read through a lengthy article, so why not create a short video that gives them the points they need to know in a short, entertaining format?

Research shows that viewers reciprocate only with video content that is relevant to their interests. A recent survey of video viewers revealed that 64% of respondents said they enjoy watching humorous videos. However, 64% of people within the same survey also said they will happily watch a video to learn more about a particular product or service, especially if it included some instructional information.

Creating the Right Videos

If you're short on time and resources, you can use Vine Video that lets you create quick and easy six-second looping videos designed to be shared across Facebook and Twitter.

Six seconds is plenty of time to show off the best features of your products or create a tantalizing sneak preview of an upcoming product launch.

Instagram Video also lets you create 15-second non-looping videos that can then be shared easily on Facebook, Twitter, Tumblr, Flickr, and Foursquare.

If you want to incorporate live video into your social media marketing strategy, Google+ Hangouts are the ideal solution. This is a great option if you're using a webcam to broadcast live or holding webinars that viewers might want to watch later. Your video can then be recorded and sent to YouTube, where it can be shared around to other networks easily just like any other YouTube video.

Circulating Your Video Content

Once you've poured all your energy into creating your video content, it's important to make sure it's circulated properly so you reach the maximum possible audience.

Uploading your videos to your YouTube channel is a logical starting point. You can share the link directly to your videos on Facebook, Twitter, and Google+ so your followers can see them easily.

Your cross channel promotion efforts need to be strategically planned and carefully considered for the individual social media network you're using.

For example, if your video is full of hashtags intended for Twitter users, don't share it on LinkedIn. Instead, consider combining your marketing efforts to appeal to the different audiences on each different site.

You might share the full video on Facebook, but only post a still image from the video to Twitter with a link for followers to click if they want to view the entire presentation.

Likewise, you might extract an interesting image from the video and overlay it with an enticing question to create a new image to upload to Instagram or Pinterest. If the viewer is curious about learning the answer to that question, they'll click through to view the entire video.

Sharing your videos on social media sites is a great way to attract attention and get people viewing your video messages, but it's important to ensure you build a solid cross channel strategy before you start blasting the exact same video all over every platform you use.

Always ensure you're using the right formats to suit your intended audience.

VIRAL MARKETING

Viral marketing is all about getting the people in your social media networks to share the things you post in their own circles. Ideally, by the time they share your content to their circle of friends or followers, you get the benefit of expanding your brand awareness to new audiences you otherwise may not have reached.

Every marketer wants to believe their message will eventually go viral. However, getting something to truly go viral is more challenging than it seems.

It's important to take into account that every social media platform is different. Content that sparks interest with your audience on one network might be completely ignored on another.

We've mentioned various social media platforms in previous chapters, but it's time now to look at the potential benefits of some individual channels you might want to incorporate into your overall strategy.

Facebook

Despite the rising popularity of various social media sites, Facebook is still king when it comes to the sheer number of users you can reach. You can share the YouTube link on your business page. Alternatively, you can upload the video directly to your business profile.

From there, Facebook allows you to promote your post directly to the people within your target audience. You can narrow down your intended audience by selecting your preferred age group, gender, location, and interests to ensure the right people are more likely to see your message.

Twitter

Twitter limits you to 140 characters, so it's important to keep your message concise. Rather than share a link to your full-length video, you may want to consider choosing a still image from the video that attracts attention.

Keep in mind that Twitter is constantly flooded with new tweets, so you need to find a way to grab your audience's attention. That's where sharing a really short, looping Vine Video can be a great tool.

Pinterest

Pinterest is the fastest growing social network, behind only Facebook and Twitter. Pinterest is entirely image based and all about visual appeal, so it's great if you incorporate images, photos, and graphics into your social media marketing strategy.

However, it's also possible to incorporate Pinterest into your video marketing strategy. Essentially you'll need to create a still image from your video, or use an interesting photo or graphic that brags attention.

You are given 500 characters to describe each picture you 'pin' to your Pinterest boards, so there's a good opportunity to add a keyword-rich description of your video.

Don't forget to put the word 'video' in the board and in your pin titles, so viewers know they can watch the full presentation if they click on the image. You can also include a call to action and hashtags to help viewers find your video.

Google+

Let's face it. If you're going to use video marketing to any extent in your social media marketing strategy, you'll need to incorporate Google+ somewhere.

Google Hangouts give you an excellent way to increase brand awareness on a couple of levels.

The first one is focused on YouTube integration. You can live stream your videos to YouTube from Google Hangouts, which automatically makes your videos appear higher on the YouTube search results pages.

The second is that Google+ (let's call it G+) can help boost your traditional search engine optimization (SEO) efforts. The SEO efforts you put into increasing website visibility should still play a role in your overall marketing strategy, so why not let Google and G+ do some of the work for you.

Essentially, Google pays attention to the interactions you receive on your content within G+. For example, you might get some comments, a few shares, and several +1s on your newest video.

Google considers that particular piece of content as being somewhat valuable, and so ranks it more favorably in search engine results.

Vine

Use Vine Video to create six second looping videos that highlight your products or offer a sneak preview of upcoming product launches. You can easily share your Vine Videos to Twitter or Facebook.

Instagram

Use Instagram Video to create 15-second videos to give a broader view of your marketing message. When you're done, Instagram allows you to share your videos across Facebook, Twitter, Tumblr, and Flickr easily.

Snapchat

It was reported in Bloomberg News back in January 2016 that Snapchat delivers more than 7 billion videos to viewers each day. When you compare that number to Facebook's reported 8 billion video views each day, it's quite a staggering figure.

It's also interesting to note that the largest demographic of users on Snapchat are millennials. An estimated 45% of users on Snapchat are millennials aged between 18 and 24, while 26% of users are aged between 25 and 34.

If you're aiming at young adult audiences, Snapchat offers plenty of opportunities to attract attention to your brand.

Take advantage of the Snapchat Story, which allows you to display a collection of short videos that can be viewed for up to 24 hours. Your viewers can reply to your video, which provides you with instant feedback from people in your audience.

Which Network To Use?

You don't have to use every single social media site out there for your social media marketing efforts to become successful. In fact, you might only want to focus on three or four as your primary marketing tools.

The key is to choose which ones have the potential to reach the right people within your target audience, and then form your marketing strategy accordingly.

Take some time to work out which social media networks are more likely to attract attention from your target audience. Then factor in your second largest demographic and match their preferred social media site accordingly.

From there, you can choose the types of media that are most likely to appeal to the people

using those social networks, which can help
your overall marketing efforts enormously.

CASE STUDIES

No matter whether you're running a brand new start-up business, or trying to expand an already-successful company, it's possible to harness the power of social media to your advantage.

The key is to look at some incredibly successful campaigns and take what you can from them to implement into your own marketing strategies.

Evian

Evian was one of the first major brands in the world to release a YouTube-exclusive marketing campaign. The 'Roller Babies' campaign showed a series of ads that featured babies enhanced by CGI programming performing crazy stunts.

Within a matter of months, each new ad in the series received millions of views.

In order to get their marketing message out there, Evian's marketing managers used a dedicated Facebook page to share their videos to followers.

Google Android: "Friends Furever"

The adorable ad for Android's "Friends Furever" campaign was the most shared video ad for all of 2015. It's nothing more than a series of clips showing unlikely animals becoming the best of friends and hanging out together.

When you think about the types of videos your own friends share on social media sites, you'll notice that around 80% of them feature animals doing something cute. So it totally made sense for Android to focus their marketing on the type of content people are already sharing.

The content is simple, but it's highly effective because it tapped into viewers' emotions. Of course, the super-cuteness of a parrot feeding spaghetti to a husky also added to the super-shareability of the video, which helped it to become a viral sensation.

Old Spice

Let's be honest here for a moment. What female doesn't want to watch a gorgeous guy with ripped muscles and tight abs doing insanely manly things while walking around half-naked commanding her attention?

For that matter, the same guy even gained the attention of a new generation of male customers. After all, the marketing team clearly understood the influence women have over men, so they used women to revive the

Old Spice product and bring it to the male target audience.

At the same time, the company managed to completely revive an old-fashioned aftershave that was reminiscent of most people's grandfather and was once associated with being a conservative brand for the older generation. Originally established back in 1934, the brand is now selling more antiperspirant, body wash, body spray, deodorant and fragrances for men than ever.

It's estimated that the wildly successful viral video campaign increased the overall revenue of Old Spice body products by 107%.
The clever marketing campaign tapped into human psychology to find a way to link their brand with being desirable, manly, and adventurous. The entire campaign implies that any man who uses Old Spice might just feel a restored feeling of manly self-esteem and become a bit of a 'lady's man' at the same time.

Of course, the ad also injected just enough subtle humor to make it super-shareable, leading the entire series to becoming a viral sensation.

Your Own Case Study

Keep in mind that each company used in the case study examples above has totally customized the marketing message to a narrow focus in order to appeal directly to the people in their respective target audiences. What works to increase sales among males aged between 25 and 34 will be completely different to the content that will drive sales from women aged between 35 and 44.

When you're working through your own marketing strategy, always keep your intended audience in mind. Then focus on the type of content, the social media network, and the specific type of media you'll use to get your message out there to your advantage.

You don't need a massive budget or a professional studio to create your videos. In fact, there are plenty of awesome programs and video creation sites out there.

All you need is to develop a fun and engaging message that appeals to your target audience – and get it out there where people can see it.

If you can get it right, chances are your business will reap the rewards in the form of a huge spike in sales.

MARKETING

The Beginners Guide to Making Money Online
with Social Media for Small Businesses

Other Available Books:

- In The Pursuit of Wisdom: The Principal Thing

- **Investing in Gold and Silver Bullion - The Ultimate Safe Haven Investments**

- Nigerian Stock Market Investment: 2 Books with Bonus Content

- **The Dividend Millionaire: Investing for Income and Winning in the Stock Market**

- Economic Crisis: Surviving Global Currency Collapse - Safeguard Your Financial Future with Silver and Gold

- **Passionate about Stock Investing: The Quick Guide to Investing in the Stock Market**

Guide to Investing in the Nigerian Stock Market

MARKETING

**The Beginners Guide to Making Money Online
with Social Media for Small Businesses**

- **Building Wealth with Dividend Stocks in the Nigerian Stock Market (Dividends - Stocks Secret Weapon)**

  - Bitcoin and Digital Currency for Beginners: The Basic Little Guide

- Child Millionaire: Stock Market Investing for Beginners - How to Build Wealth the Smart Way for Your Child

  - Christian Living: 2 Books with Bonus Content

  - **Beginners Quick Guide to Passive Income: Learn Proven Ways to Earn Extra Income in the Cyber World**

- Taming the Tongue: The Power of Spoken Words

  - **The Power of Positive Affirmations: Each Day a New Beginning**

- The Real Estate Millionaire: Beginners Quick Start Guide to Investing In

64.

Properties and Learn How to Achieve
Financial Freedom

- **Business: How to Quickly Make Real
  Money - Effective Methods to Make
  More Money: Easy and Proven Business
  Strategies for Beginners to Earn Even
  More Money in Your Spare Time**

- Money: Think Outside the Cube: 2-Book
  Money Making Boxed Set Bundle
  Strategies

If you would like to share this book with another person, please purchase an additional copy for each recipient. Thank you for your support and thanks for reading this book.

www.ingramcontent.com/pod-product-compliance
Lightning Source LLC
Chambersburg PA
CBHW051213050326
40689CB00008B/1294